Facts about Anne Heche: An American filmmaker and actor.

Stephanie M. Hudson

Copyright © Stephanie M. Hudson,2022.

Table Of Contents

Chapter One: Anne Heche's Health

According to a new agent for the actress, Anne Heche's condition has not improved since her car struck a house in Los Angeles on Friday.
Around 10:56 in the morning, LAFD arrived at the scene. According to a press statement, it took 59 firemen around 65 minutes to put out the fire and remove Heche from the driver's seat.
Witnesses told TMZ that Heche struck the neighboring house after crashing into the garage of an apartment building, then turned around and raced off.
According to KTLA, Heche was driving on Preston Way

when she allegedly ran a stop sign at the Walgrove junction and went through some sizable privacy bushes before coming to a halt inside the home.

With assistance from her neighborhood, the lady whose home was destroyed in the most recent vehicle accident involving Anne Heche is rebuilding her life.

"A spokesperson claimed over the weekend that Anne's status was stable, but that claim was false. After the accident, she slipped into a coma and has stayed there ever since "Heche's representative informed CNN in a statement on Monday.

"She needs artificial breathing due to a serious lung damage, and surgery is needed to treat burns. At the moment, she is receiving care at the Grossman Burn Center."

Heche is being looked at for a minor DUI and hit-and-run, according to LAPD Officer Annie Hernandez, CNN reported earlier on Monday.

On the day of the event, investigators secured a warrant for a blood test. Hernandez stated that they are still expecting such results. Hernandez added that the matter would be forwarded to the LA City Attorney's office once the inquiry is finished.

Heche's agent informed CNN that she had not yet been able to speak with authorities due to her injuries.

The Emmy Award winner, 53, smashed her car into the Los Angeles home on Friday, setting it ablaze. Lynne Mishele's neighbor, Lynne Bernstein, told people that the renter "was really lucky" to survive the collision without injuries.

The GoFundMe reads, "Lynne resides in the Mar Vista home that was destroyed last week by Anne Heche's automobile slamming into the property at a high rate of speed, igniting the house on fire. She lives there with her lovely puppies Bree and Rueban and tortoise Marley. "We are happy Lynne

and her family barely avoided bodily injury. But the house was destroyed by fire."
They stated that Mishele lost "her entire lifetime of things, souvenirs, all equipment for her company including her laptop and iPad, all of her clothing and basic supplies, and all home items" and that the Los Angeles Fire Department "immediately red-tagged" the residence.
CNN has approached Mishele and the Durands for comment.
As for Mishele's pets, Bernstein continues, "so were the dogs and her turtle." The woman was elsewhere in her little house when the event took place.
According to Bernstein, Mishele "was in shock" when she first spotted the car since she saw him and two other neighbors inside her home attempting to assist everyone exiting the building safely. "She may not have understood what was happening. What happened?

she questioned. What occurred? "He remembered.

A picture of Lynne Mishele was posted on a GoFundMe website created by her pals. After a car driven by Anne Heche collided with the house, she lost her home in a fire.

According to investigators, Lynne Mishele was home when Heche crashed, and a fire started. To aid Mishele in rebuilding her life, neighbors, John and Jennifer Durand have launched a GoFundMe page.

Mishele lost everything, according to the Durands' description on the fundraiser's GoFundMe page, except for a "few damaged treasured possessions." "She was able to extract a few damaged precious items from the debris with the aid of the firemen. The rest is no longer there."

Heche's automobile stopped when Roy Morgen, another Mishele neighbor, said to CNN station KCAL/KCBS,

"She was sitting two feet away from the distance.
Mishele was fortunate, according to Morgen. "She was in disbelief; it still hasn't dawned on her. Nothing remained in the home. Everything was destroyed."
"On Instagram and TikTok, the Durands invite followers to donate to the cause and help her home organizing company, Creative Organization.
A source previously told CNN that Heche has "serious burns and has a lengthy rehabilitation ahead of him."
"Her team and family are still processing what happened before the disaster," she said.

Chapter Two: Early Years of Anne Heche

The youngest of Nancy Heche's five children (née Prickett) and Donald Joseph Heche's five children, Anne Celeste Heche was born on

May 25, 1969, in Aurora, Ohio.
She's an American filmmaker and actor. Celebrity Net Worth's estimated net worth is $4 million. She made the most of her wealth working in the entertainment world for three decades, where she had success.

She achieved fame by playing identical twins Vicky Hudson and Marley Love in the soap opera Another World (1987–1991); for this role, she was honored with two Soap Opera Digest Awards and a Daytime Emmy.

She rose to fame in the late 1990s because of appearances in the drama-crime film Return to Paradise (1998), the action comedy picture Six Days, Seven Nights (1998), the horror film I Know What You Did Last Summer (1997), the disaster movie Volcano (1997), and the crime drama Donnie Brasco (1997),(1998). After receiving a Saturn Award nomination for her performance as Marion Crane in Gus Van Sant's horror

remake Psycho (1998), Heche
went on to play supporting
roles in several well-regarded
independent movies,
including Birth (2004),
Spread (2009), Cedar Rapids
(2011), Rampart (2011), and
Catfight (2012),(2016).
She drew praise for her work
on Broadway, notably
Twentieth Century, for which
she received a Tony Award
nomination, as well as for her
performance in the television
movie Gracie's Choice, for
which she received a
Primetime Emmy Award
nomination.
In addition to her film
performances, Heche has
acted in the television
comedies and dramas Men in
Trees (2006–08), Hung
(2009–11), Save Me (2013),
Aftermath (2016), and The
Brave (2017). She portrayed
Suyin Beifong in the animated
television series The Legend
of Korra (2014) and
participated in Dancing with
the Stars 29th season as a
competitor (2020).

Heche's family relocated eleven times while she was growing up, once settling in an Amish neighborhood. Heche responded, "Well, he was a choir director," when questioned about her father's income in a 2001 appearance on Larry King Live. But I doubt he earned much from that each week. Even after he passed away, he continued to claim that he was active in the gas and oil industry despite never actually doing so. At twelve, the family moved to Ocean City, New Jersey. Anne started working at a dinner theater in Swainton due to the family's tight financial situation. She recalled, "At the time, my family and I were holed up living in a bedroom at the home of a kind family from our church after being evicted from our house. "I received $100 weekly, more than anyone else in my family. After a year, we all combined our resources into a drawer-sized envelope and accumulated enough money to move away.

When Heche was 13 years old, her 45-year-old father passed away on March 3, 1983, from HIV/AIDS, which she thought he had acquired from a gay partner: "He was in total denial until the day he died. We know that his gay connections are where he got it. Absolutely. It wasn't just one, in my opinion. We were aware of his lifestyle at the time because he was a very promiscuous man, Heche stated on Larry King Live. Heche said that he routinely sexually assaulted her from the time she was a baby until she was 12 years old, inflicting genital herpes on her.

In a 2001 interview with The Advocate, Heche was questioned, "But why would a homosexual guy rape a girl?" to which she responded, "I don't think he was just a gay man. I believe he had sexual promiscuity. I thought my father had to hide the fact that he was gay. I believe he was sexually violent. The more it poured out of him in [the] ways that it did, the more he struggled to be who he was. She remarked in a 1998 interview that her father had been eventually hidden and "destroyed both our family and his happiness. I did learn how to tell the truth, though. Nothing else has any value." Heche's 18-year-old brother Nathan was fatally injured three months after her father passed away in a vehicle accident. It was determined that he hit a tree after falling asleep at the wheel, but Heche believes it was a suicide.] Heche attended the forward-thinking Francis W. Parker School in Chicago when the rest of her family relocated there.

At 16, Heche was cast in the daytime soap opera As the World Turns when an agent saw her in a school play. Heche traveled to New York City, attended an audition, and received a job offer; nevertheless, her mother demanded she complete high school first. Heche was

allowed to play two characters in the daytime soap opera Another World just before she graduated from high school in 1987.
"Again, I was denied entry. My mother was quite devout and perhaps believed that the world was full of sinners, "Heche said. "But I called and requested that they send me the ticket. I'm boarding the aircraft. I yelled, "Bye!" I finished my sentence with my mother in a filthy one-bedroom apartment."

Chapter Three: Personal life

Heche's romance with Ellen DeGeneres and what transpired after it ended attracted much media attention. The pair began dating in 1997 and once declared they would enter into a civil union if it were made legal in Vermont. It ended in August 2000. Heche has acknowledged that all of her prior love partnerships have included men.

On September 1, 2001, Heche married Coleman "Coley" Laffoon, a cinematographer she had met the year before on DeGeneres' stand-up comedy tour, after allegedly splitting up with DeGeneres for him in 2000. Their son is born. After being married for five and a half years, Laffoon filed for divorce on February 2, 2007. March 4, 2009, marked the finalization of the divorce.

Heche allegedly deserted her spouse for James Tupper, a co-star in Men in Trees. On December 5, 2008, Heche's agent announced that the actress was expecting their son, who would be both her and his first child. In 2018, Tupper and Heche divorced.

Family

Three of Heche's four siblings have passed away.

Susan passed away from brain cancer.

She and Heche were no longer close.

A cardiac abnormality caused
Cynthia's death in infancy.
Just before Nathan graduated
from high school, he was
killed in an automobile
accident. His death, according
to Anne, was a suicide.
Abigail and Nancy Heche, her
mother
Since Heche confronted
Nancy about the alleged
sexual assault she claimed to
have experienced at the hands
of her father, Heche and
Nancy have been on bad
terms. Heche said in her 2001
autobiography, Call Me Crazy,
that her mother misdiagnosed
her baby's genital herpes as a
diaper rash and failed to take
her to the doctor.
In response to her daughter's
accusations, Nancy said, "I am
attempting to create a place
for myself in this writing, a
place where I as Anne's
mother do not feel violated or
scandalized." Nancy was
horrified by her daughter's
accusations. She said, "Among
the falsehoods and
blasphemies on these pages, I
find no place."

"It is my opinion that my sister Anne truly believes, at this moment, what she has asserted about our father's past behavior," Heche's jewelry designer sister Abigail continued. "However, at the same time, I would like to point out that Anne, in the past, has expressed doubts herself about the accuracy of such memories." She stated: "I think her memories of our father are false based on my experience and her own voiced misgivings. And regardless of Anne's opinions, I can categorically affirm that the claim that our mother was aware of such activity is untrue."

Heche claims that Nancy's brother Nathan committed suicide. Still, Nancy refutes this, saying, "I have talked to his youth pastor, and he said that Nathan was committed to the Lord, he loved Jesus, and I do not believe that that was suicide, but the death of his father from homosexuality three months earlier could have certainly stirred up a lot of confusion for him."

Since her spouse passed away from AIDS, Nancy has worked as a Christian therapist and motivational speaker. She gives talks on "overcoming homosexuality" for James Dobson's Focus on the Family.

Anne Heche stated to The New York Times in 2009, "My mother's life was quite terrible. Her spouse and three of her five children have both passed away. I believe that she is trying to hide the agony of reality by trying to convert homosexual people into straight people. People sometimes ask me why I am so honest about the events in my life, and the answer is because, for better or worse, the falsehoods I have been exposed to and the denial I have grown up in have given birth to a child of honesty and love.

Even now, the reverse of that basic value is what my mother promotes. She continues to fight against love, and this is not a mistake. One also questions why I'm delaying having her meet my children". Heche said to The Daily Telegraph in 2011 that she doesn't think she would ever be able to mend her connection with her mother.

mental illness

Heche traveled from Los Angeles to Cantua Creek outside of Fresno, California, on August 19, 2000, and parked her Toyota SUV alongside a barren roadside. Heche traveled 2.4 kilometers (1.2 miles) into the desert wearing nothing but a bra and shorts before knocking on a stranger's ranch house.] Araceli Campiz, the house's resident, answered the door and immediately saw Heche from the movie Six Days, Seven Nights. She walked in as Campiz was thinking, "Oh my God, we're in the middle of nowhere," he remembered. Heche downed glass after glass of water, according to Campiz, and then "ripped off her Nikes and stated she needed to take a shower," to which Campiz complied and extended a towel to Heche. Heche was not intoxicated, under the influence of drugs, or unwell as far as Campiz could tell; nonetheless, Heche subsequently acknowledged having used ecstasy. Heche took a shower, sat in the living room, asked for some slippers, and advised Campiz to do the same. According to Campiz, "She wanted to watch a movie, but the VCR was broken." After being first perplexed by Heche's lack of movement for a half hour—doing neither contacting pals nor a garage—Campiz got worried.

According to Campiz, "I didn't know what to do. I then made a call to the sheriff's office. According to a police report on KSEE-TV, Heche informed the deputies that she was "God" and would transport everyone to paradise in a spacecraft when they arrived. Heche was transported by ambulance the 50 miles (80 km) to Fresno's University Medical Center by the deputies, where she was hospitalized in the mental unit and later released. Heche said that for the first 31 years of her life, she was "crazy" and that her father's sexual assault of her as a kid and infant caused this. Heche said on national television that she created a fantasy world called the "Fourth Dimension" to make herself feel safe and that she had an alter ego which was the daughter of God and half-sister of Jesus Christ named "Celestia" who had contact with extraterrestrial life forms in a series of interviews with Barbara Walters, Matt Lauer, and Larry King to promote Call Me Crazy in 2001. Following the event at Cantua Creek, Heche said she overcame her mental health issues and has left her alter ego behind.

car accident

Heche was engaged in a series of two vehicle accidents on August 5, 2022, in the Los Angeles neighborhood of Mar Vista; she suffered severe burns both times she crashed, first when the Mini Cooper she was driving into a garage at an apartment complex, and again when she struck a home. Heche was carried away from the collision scene in KTTV's video from Los Angeles. Heche was brought to a hospital, and soon after, the Los Angeles Fire Department issued a statement indicating that Heche was in serious condition.

 Later, according to Brian Humphrey of the Los Angeles Fire Department, the car compromised the home's structure, and it took 59 firemen 65 minutes to put out the fire and free Heche from the vehicle. The homeowner was in the house's backyard at the time of the collision and was not injured.
Heche's podcast co-host Heather Duffy Boylston informed the Associated Press on August 7 that Heche's condition was stable.
According to law enforcement officials, according to a

statement to the Los Angeles Times, Heche was "deemed to be under the influence and acting strangely" at the time of the collisions. A spokesperson for Heche claimed on August 8 that Heche was in a coma and needed medical care due to a lung injury.

 Heche is believed to have been impaired by alcohol in both incidents, so police sought a search order for her blood work from the hospital after the collision. If it is proven that Heche was under the influence of drugs or alcohol, she might be charged with minor DUI and hit-and-run.

Chapter Four: Career and Media

Around 1990
Heche won the 1991 Daytime Emmy for Outstanding Younger Actress in a Drama Series for her role in Another World. Heche debuted on

primetime television in a
Murphy Brown episode in
November 1991. The following
year, she made her TV movie
debut with a brief cameo in
the Hallmark Hall of Fame
production of O Pioneers!
(1992).

Heche made her feature film
debut in 1993 alongside Elijah
Wood in Disney's The
Adventures of Huck Finn. She
played modest supporting
roles in made-for-TV films,
including Girls in Prison
(1994) and Kingfish: A Story
of Huey P. Long during the
next two years (1995). She
also played Joan Chen's
lesbian lover in the 1995
straight-to-video
pornographic thriller Wild
Side.

In a portion of the made-for-
HBO anthology film If These
Walls Could Talk, which also
starred Cher and Demi
Moore, Heche had her first
significant acting role as a
college girl considering
abortion in 1996. In the indie
film Walking and Talking, she
co starred with Catherine

Keener in the part of childhood best friends. The restricted release movie received positive reviews from reviewers and ranked 47 on Entertainment Weekly's list of the "Top 50 Cult Films of All-Time." Heche received a commendation from Austin Chronicle film writer Alison Macor, who stated in her assessment that she "is destined for greater cinematic roles." In the 1997 crime film Donnie Brasco, she portrayed the wife of Johnny Depp's eponymous FBI undercover agent. The New York Times reviewer Janet Maslin said that "[Heche] does well with what could have been the thankless part" in her review of the $124.9 million-grossing movie.

Heche continued to enjoy critical acclaim and financial success by the late 1990s when she accepted supporting roles in three more high-profile 1997 films: Wag the Dog, Volcano, and I Know What You Did Last Summer. She co-starred in Volcano, a catastrophe movie about a volcano erupting in Los Angeles, alongside Tommy Lee Jones and Gaby Hoffmann, who played a seismologist.

Although the film received mixed reviews from critics, it brought in US$122 million at the international box office. In the slasher horror sleeper smash I Know What You Did Last Summer, she played a small part as a rural solitary, featuring Ryan Phillippe, Sarah Michelle Gellar, Jennifer Love Hewitt, and Freddie Prinze Jr. Heche was praised by various reviews, including Variety, despite having a small role in the movie.

In the political farce Wag the Dog, she landed the part of a presidential advisor alongside Robert De Niro and Dustin Hoffman, even though the job was initially intended for a male. The movie grossed US$64 million against a US$15 million budget.

Heche's first leading part was in the 1998 romantic fantasy

Six Days, Seven Nights. She co-starred with Harrison Ford and played a New York City journalist who ended up on a remote island with a pilot (Ford) due to a plane disaster. One day before her same-sex relationship with Ellen DeGeneres became widely known, she had been cast in the movie.

Although Heche was soon cast in a second leading role opposite Vince Vaughn in the drama Return to Paradise (1998), she believed that her romance with DeGeneres had damaged her chances of landing a big part. People told him, "You're not getting a job because you're homosexual," according to Heche. How could it ruin my career, she asked? I'm still having trouble comprehending it.

Despite mixed reviews, Six Days, Seven Nights made US$74.3 million in North America and US$164.8 million globally. A writer for The New York Times remarked about Anne Heche's role in the dramatic thriller

Return to Paradise: "Return to Paradise takes on the abstract weightiness of an ethical debate rather than the visceral urgency of a thriller, as Ms. Heche's formidable Beth Eastern does her best to manipulate the other characters on [co-star Joaquin Phoenix's character behalf."
]'s
Heche played the lead role in Gus Van Sant's 1998 adaptation of Alfred Hitchcock's 1960 film Psycho. She assumed the part initially performed by Janet Leigh, Marion Crane, an embezzler who checks into a run-down motel owned and operated by a serial murderer named Norman Bates, in the revised version (played by Vince Vaughn in their second collaboration). Despite a US$60 million budget, Psycho received unfavorable reviews and only produced a meager US$37.1 million worldwide. According to Janet Maslin of The New York Times, Heche was "refreshingly cast in Marion's part," and noted that

her performance was "nearly as modest as Ms. Leigh's, yet she's also more assertive and flirtatious." She has only ever had a leading part in her 1998 films, which have all been theatrically released.

Around 2000

She portrayed the part of Dr. Sterling in the movie adaption of Elizabeth Wurtzel's memoirs about depression, Prozac Nation, which starred Christina Ricci and Jessica Lange. She worked in indie films and television roles for most of the early 2000s. The movie, which had its world premiere at the 2001 Toronto International Film Festival, was released on DVD in 2005. In the suspense film John Q, she played a hospital administrator who worked with a father and husband (Denzel Washington) whose son was identified as having an enlarged heart. Despite receiving unfavorable reviews from critics, the project brought in $102.2 million at the global box office. She was also given a recurring part in the fourth season of the Ally McBeal television show in 2001.

Heche made her Broadway debut in 2002 as a young lady who had inherited her father's mathematical prowess and mental instability in staging the Pulitzer Prize-winning drama Proof. Heche was deemed by The New York Times to be "Ms. Heche, whose stage experience is limited and who is making her New York stage debut at 33, plays the part with a more appealing ear and more conventional timing; her interpretation of the character is equally viable.

The reviewer compared her to Mary-Louise Parker and Jennifer Jason Leigh, who had previously played her character in other productions of the play. Her Catherine has signs of delayed development and is hurried, angry, and impulsive ".

Heche was nominated for both a Saturn Award for Best Actress and a Primetime

Emmy Award for Best Supporting Actress in 2004 for her roles in the Lifetime films Gracie's Choice and The Dead Will Tell, respectively. She co-starred with Alec Baldwin in the same year's Broadway production of Twentieth Century, which tells the story of a brilliant and egotistical Broadway director (Baldwin) who turns a chorus girl (Heche) into a leading lady. She received a nomination for the 2004 Tony Award for Best Actress in a Play for her performance. She starred in the acclaimed indie drama Birth in 2004 with Nicole Kidman and Cameron Bright.

In the 2004–2005 season of the WB drama Everwood, she took on a recurring role as a mafia wife who needs reconstructive surgery. In 2005, she played the same character on Nip/Tuck the following year. Heche resumed her career in television with roles in the made-for-CBS film Silver Bells (2005) and the made-for-Lifetime film Fatal Desire, in which she played a con artist who conned a guy she met online (2006).

Heche co-starred with Azura Skye and Elizabeth Banks in the small-scale dramedy Sexual Life (2005), which was about contemporary romance. The movie had its broadcast premiere in addition to screenings at film festivals. Heche started production on her series, Men in Trees, in 2006. After learning that her engaged partner is having an affair, she played a New York novelist who relocates to a tiny Alaskan village where there are many single men and few women. The season of Men in Trees was cut short by the writer's strike, which was canceled in May 2008. Heche appeared in three films that were released when the program was aired but received little attention from viewers: the romantic comedy What Love Is (2007), the science-fiction thriller Toxic Skies (2008), and the horror-

comedy Suffering Man's
Charity (2007).
Heche co-starred with Ashton
Kutcher in the 2009 sex
comedy Spread as the
girlfriend of a narcissistic
gigolo. The movie only had a
small run in North American
cinemas, but it earned US$12
million at the global box
office. According to Matthew
Turney of View London,
Heche provides "tremendous
support" in this "enjoyable,
brilliantly written, and
wonderfully photographed LA
drama." Additionally, in
2009, she was chosen to play
the ex-wife of a high school
baseball and basketball coach
in the HBO comedy series
Hung (portrayed by Thomas
Jane). The show aired
through 2011 and garnered
positive reviews.

Around 2010

A much more significant role
in the independent comedy
Cedar Rapids (2011), in which
she played a seductive
insurance agent with whom a
naive and idealistic man
(played by Ed Helms) falls in

love, followed her cameo appearance as the CEO of a significant company in the well-received comedy The Other Guys (2010), starring Will Ferrell and Mark Wahlberg.

The Sundance premiere production received positive reviews and was a hit with the arthouse crowd. While Heche works most acceptable in a more brittle mode, as in HBO's Hung, she achieves a beautiful balance between Joan's impish and maternal sides, according to David Rooney in The Hollywood Reporter's review of the movie.
She co-starred in the 2011 drama Rampart starring Woody Harrelson and Cynthia Nixon, as one of the two sisters who were the spouses of a dishonest police officer (Harrelson). Following its premiere at the 36th Toronto International Film Festival, the movie had a limited theatrical release and received favorable reviews.

The San Francisco Chronicle
noted Heche and her other
female co-stars, saying they
"allow Harrelson to shine —
he has always had a way of
preening for women — and he
brings out the best in
them."Heche starred in the
Sundance Film Festival-
premiered comedy That's
What She Said (2012) and the
highly praised dramedy
Arthur Newman, in which she
portrayed the girlfriend of a
former professional golfer
(Colin Firth) (also 2012).
In the supernatural horror
film Nothing Left to Fear
(2013), Heche co-starred with
James Tupper, Jennifer
Stone, and Rebekah Brandes
as a family. An unstable
clergyman disrupts their lives
in a new town. The movie was
made available on VOD and in
a few theaters. The Los
Angeles Times stated that
both Heche and Tupper
"should compose apologetic
emails to their supporters"
after it received negative
reviews.

Additionally, in 2013, Heche played a Midwestern housewife who thinks she communicates with God in the short-lived NBC comedy Save Me. In the action film Wild Card, she portrayed the waitress companion of a Jason Statham character who was a recovering gambler (2014).

 Despite having a $30 million budget and only receiving a limited theatrical distribution in some regions of North America, the movie only made US$6.7 million abroad. Before it was canceled, she had a regular guest spot on The Michael J. Fox Show. She agreed to a first-look agreement with Universal Television in 2013.

Heche played the chief of the FBI office in Jerusalem in the USA Network action-adventure drama series Dig, where investigators discovered a 2,000-year-old conspiracy while looking into an archaeologist's death. Late in 2014, the six-episode series made its debut.

Heche had a special appearance as Dr. Susan Langdon, a criminal profiler, on the ABC drama Quantico in 2015. Aftermath, a post-apocalyptic action drama starring Heche, had its television premiere on September 27, 2016, on Syfy in the United States and Canada. Heche portrayed Karen Copeland, an Air Force pilot from Washington who, with her husband Josh, a university professor co-producer of the series, and their three almost adult children, must survive Armageddon. Dig and Aftermath were not given a second season.

Heche and Topher Grace starred in the 2016 film Opening Night, which included Heche in a supporting role as the lead vocalist for a Broadway musical. The Los Angeles Film Festival had a screening of the musical comedy. Heche co-starred with Sandra Oh in the 2016 indie comedy Catfight, about two enmity-filled rivals pursuing a lifelong vendetta. Like Heche's other cinematic endeavors, the movie had a limited distribution and a VOD debut before mainly receiving positive reviews from reviewers. According to the Los Angeles Times: "Oh and Heche act admirably in this scene, completely lacking in conceit and self-consciousness.

They aren't afraid to be crude, which makes them hilarious because of how they treat others around them and the bruises they leave behind after fights. Heche portrays Joyce, the mentally ill mother of the teenage Jeffrey Dahmer (Ross Lynch), in the 2017 film My Friend Dahmer. The Hollywood Reporter and Empire praised her for her portrayal, calling it "nerve-jangling excellence" and "entertainingly off-kilter." Heche made her acting debut in the brand-new military/espionage thriller The Brave on September 25, 2017, as (fictitious) Deputy

Director Patricia Campbell of the (actual) Defense Intelligence Agency, or the "DIA." Heche is the star of this NBC series, which runs from 2017 to 2018. Mike Vogel, the male team leader, commands an elite group of professionals from several military branches who are required to complete hazardous missions.

She began appearing in a supporting role on the television show Chicago P.D. in 2018.

Around 2020

Heche was revealed to be one of the famous contestants on the 29th Dancing with the Stars season on September 2, 2020.

Media

She has featured on the covers of several magazines throughout her career, including Entertainment Weekly, Mirabella, and Observer Magazine. In 1998, People magazine named Heche one of the 50 Most Beautiful People in the World. While dating comedian Ellen

DeGeneres, she attracted considerable media attention. In 2017, Heche and Jason Ellis co-hosted the Love and Heche radio program on SiriusXM.

Chapter Five: Nominations and Awards

Year Title Award Category Result
1989 Soap Opera Digest Awards Outstanding Female Newcomer - Daytime Winner
1989 Another World Daytime Emmy Awards Outstanding Younger Actress in a Drama Series Nominee
Outstanding Younger Actress in a Drama Series at the 1991 Daytime Emmy Awards
Great Lead Actress in a Daytime Drama, 1992 Soap Opera Digest Awards
Nominated for Best Supporting Actress in a Motion Picture at the 1997 Wag the Dog Satellite Awards

1999 Saturn Awards Best
Supporting Actress
Nomination Fangoria
Chainsaw Awards Best
Actress Nomination 1998
Psycho Golden Raspberry
Awards Worst Supporting
Actress Nomination 1999 Six
Days, Seven Nights Herself
Nominated for 2000's
Blockbuster Entertainment
Awards Favorite Actress -
Comedy/Romance Awards
given by GLAAD Winning the
Stephen F. Kolzak Award
Lucy Awards for Women in
Film Lucy Award Won
Nominated for Outstanding
Supporting Actress in a
Miniseries or a Movie at the
2004 Gracie's Choice
Primetime Emmy Awards
Nominated for a 2004 The
Dead Will Tell Saturn Award
for Best Television Actress
Nominated for a 2004
Twentieth Century Tony
Award for Best Actress in a
Play

Chapter 6: Literature and Cinema

Book

The voice actor for Call Me Crazy: A Memoir is Anne Heche (2001). Simon & Schuster, New York. OCLC 47243952, ISBN 9780743216890.

Film

The year 1993, the role, and the accompanying notes. An Attack by Ghosts Denise
The Huck Finn Adventures Elizabeth Wilks
1994 I'll Take Any Action Claire A Punctual Turn of Events Tanny's Companion Dairy Money Betty
 1995 Crazy Side
 1996 Alex Lee Juliet, the Juror Pie in the Sky Amy, Moving and Speaking Laura
1997 Toby Brasco Volcano Maggie Pistone Amy Barnes, D.O.
I am aware of your summertime activities. Missy" Melissa Egan
Dog Whistle Winning Ames

1998 Seven Days and Six Days
Howard Monroe
Going back to paradise Psycho
Beth McBride
1999, Marion Crane Threefold
Miracle Roxane
2000 August Rose Linda
Brown Beyond Suspicion
2001 is another name for
fluoxetine Nation, Dr. Sterling
2002 John Q. Jennifer Payne
birth of Clara in 2004 Sex Life
Gwen
2007 Man's Charity in
Suffering Jacobsen, Helen
Laura Superman's What Love
Is: Doomsday The Lois Lane
Voice
2008 Sky pollution Tess
Martin, M.D.
2009 Distribution Samantha
2010 The Others Boardman,
Pamela Uncredited
2011 Wood Rapids Rampart
Joan Ostrowski-Fox
2012 Catherine She said it like
that. Black Dee Dee
November Barbra
A. N. Newman Crawley, Mina
2013 Nothing to fear
anymore, Wendy
With These Speeds, Life
Coach Rowan

2014 Insane Card 2016 Roxy
Premiere Night Catfight with
Brooke Ashley Reaction Riley
The Final Word
2019 Elizabeth The Nicest of
Opponents
2020 Mary Ellis The Missing
Ingrid Michaelson
2021 13.0 minutes Tammy

Television

Year Title Role Notes
1987–91 Another Planet
Marley Love and Vicky
Hudson 1991 cast member
McGill Brown NICO Episode 1
1992 Dear Pioneers! Marie TV
movie
1993 The Adventures of
Young Indiana Jones Kate,
episode one
1994 With the Wall Sharon TV
movie
Female Prisoners The
Investigator Jennifer Lucinda
Short
1995 Kingfish: A Story of
Huey P. Long, a TV movie
starring Aileen Dumont
1996 When These Walls Talk,
Television movie starring
Christine Cullen; "1996" 1997
1998's Subway Stories:

Pregnant Girl TV Movie,
"Manhattan Miracle" segment
One episode of Ellen Karen
2000 TV movie One Kill Capt.
Mary Jane O'Malley
2001 Toby McBeal Theodora
West six episodes
2004 Gracie's Decision
Lawson, Rowena TV movie
Emily Parker will learn from
the dead.
2004–05 Everwood Jessica
Hayes ten shows
2005 True Rosie True Pilot
not yet aired
Nip/Tuck Three episodes of
Nicole Morretti
Gold Bells Hallmark film
starring Catherine O'Mara
2005–06 Heroes of
Higglytown The waitress
Gloria (voice) three shows
A Fatal Desire (2006) Tanya
Sullivan television movie
Masters of Science Fiction
2007 One episode of Martha
Van Vogel
Men in Trees, 2006–2008 36
episodes; series leader Marin
Frist
Lead part in Toxic Skies
(2008)

2009-11 Hung Jessica Haxon,
30 episodes; lead part
2011 Girl Fight Melissa
television movie
Silent Witness (2011) Robb,
Kate
2012 Power Outage Debra
Westen, M.D. Miniseries
2012 Save Me 2013 Beth
Harper, 7 episodes in the lead
role
2013–14 Michael J. Fox's TV
program episodes of Susan
Rodriguez-Jones
Adventure Time 2013–2015
Soda Cherry Cream (voice)
Episodes 2
One Christmas Eve in 2014
Hallmark movie starring Nell
Blackemore
the Korra legend by Suyin
Beifong (voice) Seasons 3 and
4 recurring role
2015 Dig Monahan, Lynn
Mini Series\Quantico Susan
Langdon, MD one episode
2016's consequences
Copeland, Karen 10 attacks;
series opener
Carol from A Christmas Carol
Hallmark Movie 2017–18
Patricia Campbell, DIA deputy
director for The Brave leading

series 2018–2019 Superintendent of the Chicago Police Department Katherine Brennan Regular role Sixth season; Guests 11 episodes in Season 7

2020 The Stars of Dancing Herself a participant in season 29 in 2021 Each Rise 2 episodes of Corrine Cuthbert 2022–present TBD: The Idol Regular role

Direction

(2000) Year Title Notes Segment 2 of If These Walls Could Talk: "2000" and "2001" Reaching Normal, an On the Edge segment from the American Summer Documentary with Ellen DeGeneres